Wool from Sheep

Julie Haydon

Chapter 1
What Is Wool?

Wool is the soft, curly hair or fur that grows on some animals.

We use wool to make:

clothes

blankets

carpets

2

Why do people like woolen clothes?

Woolen clothes:
- keep a person warm
- feel soft and light
- keep their shape
- are hard to burn

3

Chapter 2

Wool from Sheep

Most of the wool we use comes from sheep.
Sheep live on farms.

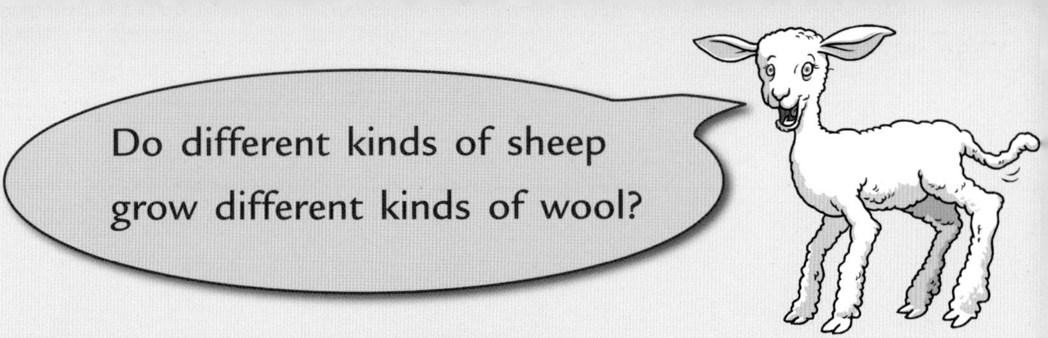
Do different kinds of sheep grow different kinds of wool?

Some wool is thinner than others,
and some wool is longer than others.
Most sheep grow white wool,
but some sheep grow wool of other colors.

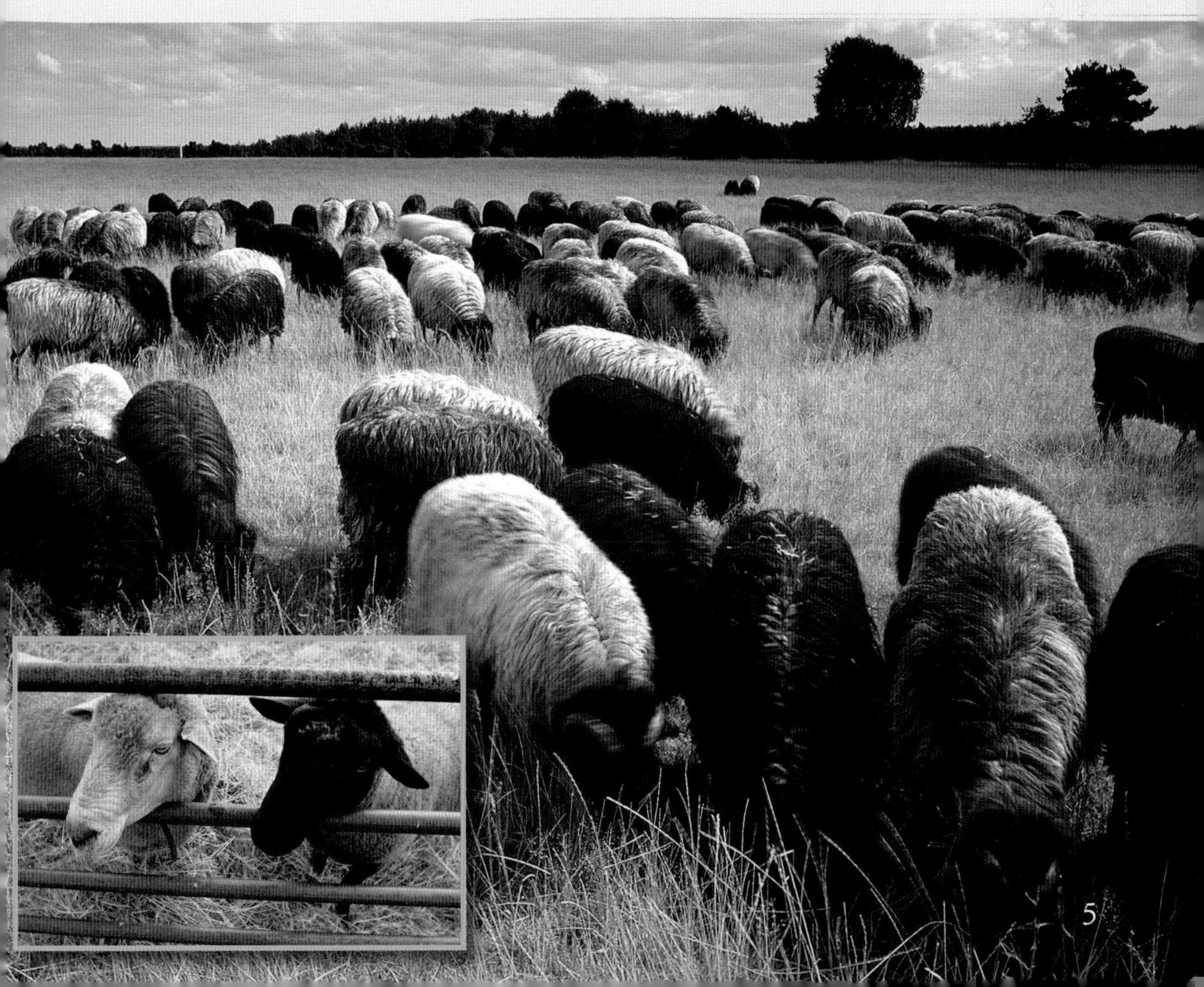

Chapter 3
Feeding Sheep

Sheep live on farms.
They eat grass and other plants
that grow in the fields.
Sometimes farmers give their sheep other food,
such as hay.
Sheep drink lots of water, too.

sheep eating hay

Are sheep just called sheep?

A baby sheep is called a lamb.

A female sheep is called a ewe.

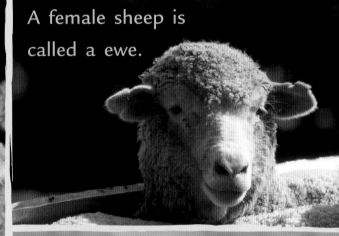

A male sheep is called a ram.

Chapter 4

Healthy Sheep

Farmers want healthy sheep,
so they give their sheep medicine.
Some medicine keeps the sheep
safe from **diseases**.
Some medicine kills the worms
that live inside sheep.

a farmer giving
his sheep medicine

Why do farmers have to check their sheep?

Farmers look and feel
for anything that might
hurt their sheep or make them sick.

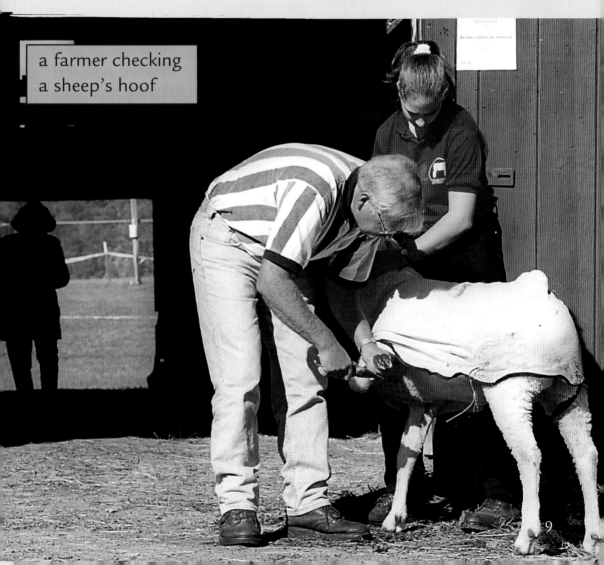

a farmer checking
a sheep's hoof

9

Chapter 5
Baths for Sheep

Some insects live in sheep's wool.
The insects can bite the sheep
and make them sick.
Farmers give their sheep special baths called **dips**.
This kills the insects.

How does dipping work?

The sheep swim through a deep pool.
There are **chemicals** in the pool.
The chemicals kill the insects
that live in the sheep's wool.

This sheep has just been through a dip.

11

Herding the Sheep

Sometimes the sheep must be moved
from one place to another.
The sheep are gathered and moved together.
This is called herding the sheep.

How does a farmer herd sheep?

The farmer follows behind the sheep.
The farmer may walk, ride a horse,
or ride a motorcycle.
Many farmers have dogs
that help them herd the sheep.
The dogs do not hurt the sheep.

Chapter 7
Shearing the Sheep

Sheep grow wool over most of their bodies.
Once or twice a year
the wool is cut off the sheep.
This is called shearing the sheep.

What is a sheep's coat called?

Its coat is called a **fleece**.

The fleece is cut off a sheep in one piece.

fleece

Chapter 8

Shearers

People who shear sheep are called shearers.
Shearers work in shearing sheds.
A shearer uses a small machine
to shear the sheep.
The shearer holds the machine in one hand.

How long does it take to shear a sheep?

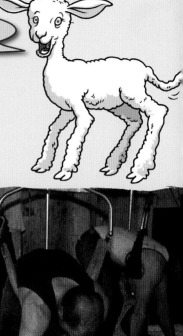

It takes about three minutes.
A fast shearer can shear
about 200 sheep in a day.

Chapter 9

The Fleeces

The fleeces are sorted in the shed and put into large bags called bales. The bales of wool are sent away to be sold. Then the bales go to a factory.

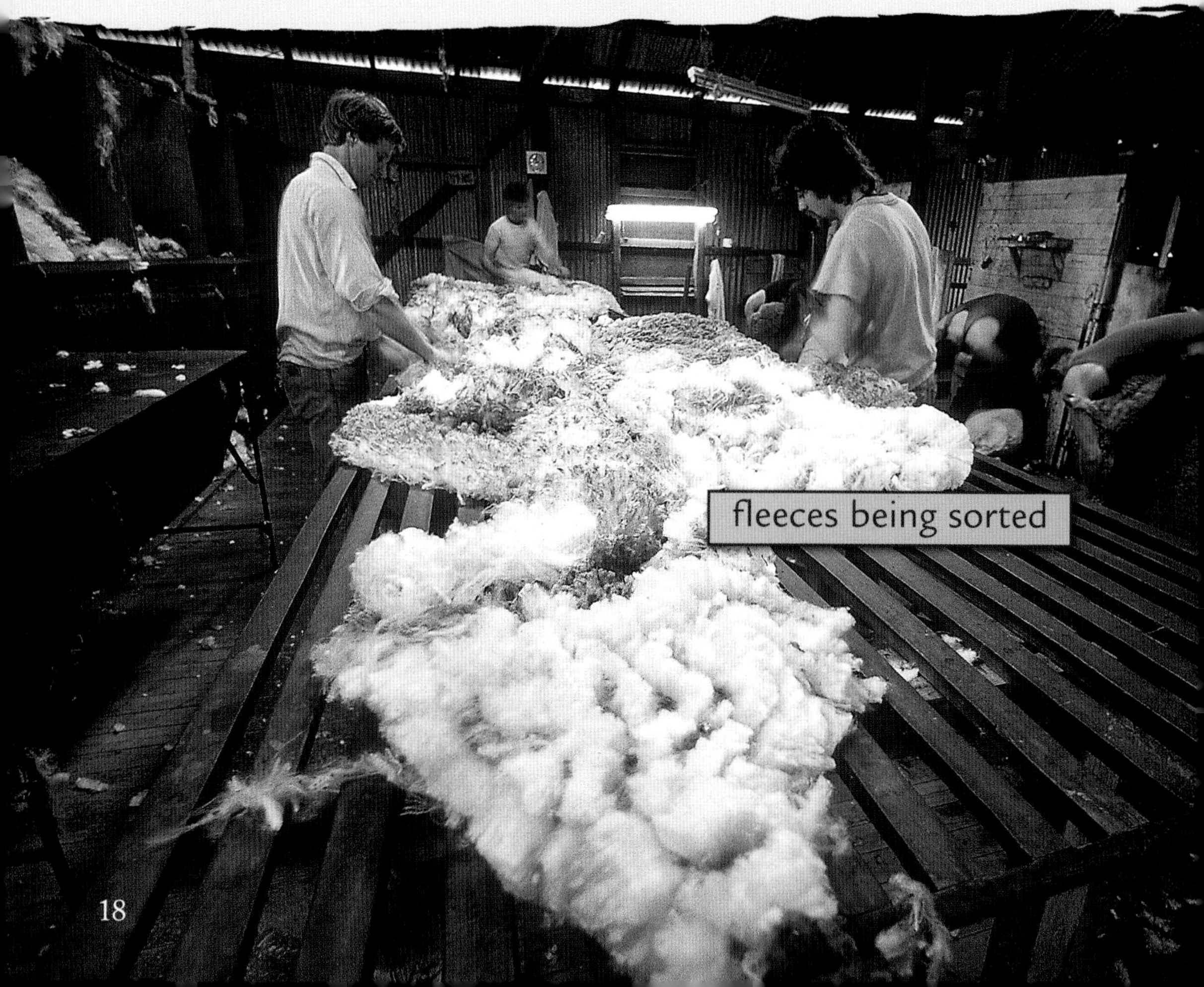

fleeces being sorted

Are fleeces clean?

Fleeces are full of dirt, seeds, and oil.

Chapter 10
At the Factory

At the factory, the fleeces are sorted,
washed, and dried.
Machines comb out the wool.
Then the wool is **spun** into yarn.

What color is yarn?

Yarn can be **dyed** many colors.

Chapter 11
Yarn

Yarn is used to make fabric for clothes, blankets, and carpets.

Yarn is made into fabric on machines. People can make fabric by hand, too.

What does a person need to start knitting?

Some yarn and two knitting needles are needed.

Glossary

chemicals   substances that are often mixed with another substance, such as water, to change them

dips   baths of chemicals given to sheep to kill the insects that live in sheep's wool

diseases   sicknesses

dyed   has color added to it

fleece   the woolen coat of a sheep, which is shorn off in one piece

spun   twisted

Index